THE GREEK NEWS

ANTON POWELL & PHILIP STEELE

Dear Reader,

Here at THE GREEK NEWS, we've been looking through past copies of our newspaper to find the stories that really made the headlines. And we've asked our best reporters to rewrite them specially for this edition.

You'll find news stories on all the truly great events that took place within our history, along with fascinating articles on everyday life — our feasts and fashions, our theater, our gods and wars, and lots, lots more.

We hope you have just as much fun reading THE GREEK NEWS as we've had putting it together.

The Editors in Chief

Anton Powell   Philip Steele

A NOTE FROM OUR PUBLISHER

As we all know, the ancient Greeks didn't really have newspapers.
But if they had, we're sure that they would have been reading *The Greek News*!
We hope you enjoy it.

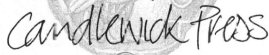

CANDLEWICK PRESS
CAMBRIDGE, MASSACHUSETTS

CONTENTS

Map of Greece

THRACE

MACEDONIA

Mount Olympus

Aegean Sea

THESSALY

Lampsacus

LESBOS

Ionian Sea

Thermopylae

Delphi

ATTICA

Eretria

Marathon

Thebes

LYDIA

PELOPONNESE

Athens

Ephesus

Olympia

Corinth

Priene

Mycenae

Miletus

Epidaurus

SALAMIS

Sparta

N
W — E
S

COS

SANTORINI

RHODES

Mediterranean Sea

EUROPE

ASIA

AFRICA

CRETE

Map by GILLIAN TYLER

NEW BEGINNINGS

Illustrated by CHRIS FORSEY

TRAVEL TO NORTH AFRICA and you'll find people speaking Greek. Travel to Italy or southern France and it's the same story! But how did this come about? *The Greek News* looks back to the days when some of our people set sail for faraway places.

NOW, WE ALL know our homeland is the finest in the world. But let's face it, Greece *is* a country of mountains and islands. There just isn't a lot of good farmland.

And because each of our cities rules only a small area, it either has to grow all its own food or be wealthy enough to trade for it.

Long ago, between 750 and 500 B.C., many city-states had become too big to feed all their people.

So some Greeks were forced to leave their cities to look for new lands, where they could settle and build colonies.

These brave pioneers headed off in every direction, setting up new homes as far away as North Africa, the Black Sea coast, and even Spain.

PACK UP YOUR TROUBLES

But just who were these settlers? Often, they were people who were down on their luck—short of land and possessions.

Some colonists were led by noblemen who'd argued with their rulers.

GO AWAY! Angry islanders on Santorini throw stones at the returning colonists.

The Spartan prince named Dorieus was a typical case. In about 520 B.C., after his rival won the Spartan throne, Dorieus sailed off in a fury to start a colony in North Africa.

But not all colonists were adventurers like Dorieus. On the island of Santorini, where people were starving, the young men were given a simple choice: "Sail off to North Africa—or face death!"

The men left their homeland and struggled to build a colony in Africa. But their new life was so hard that in the end they gave up and headed back home.

They didn't get a warm welcome, though—the people of Santorini threw stones to drive them away. There was nothing the

colonists could do but return to Africa.

But this story does have a happy ending— their colony eventually became the thriving city of Cyrene.

FORTUNES FROM FAR AWAY

At first, our colonies provided new places for people to live. But they soon became vital in other ways as well.

Where would we be without the grain and metals they supply? Not to mention all those important luxuries—gold, ivory, perfumes . . .

Long may all of our colonies prosper!

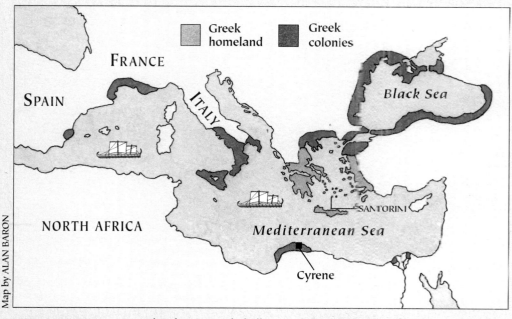

NEW HOMES: Brave Greek colonists settled all around the Mediterranean Sea.

Map by ALAN BARON

TYRANTS OUT!

Illustrated by RON TINER

ATHENS HASN'T ALWAYS been the powerful city-state it is today. In the 500s B.C., it was just one small state among many. Then the people of Athens threw out their tyrant and took the government into their own hands.

THE CHANGE began in 528 B.C., when control of the city passed to the all-powerful tyrant, Hippias.

Hippias inherited the city from his father, Pisistratus, who was remembered as a good and fair leader — despite ruling as a tyrant.

At first, Hippias also governed fairly. Then, in 514 B.C., things changed.

Two Athenian noble-men, named Harmodius and Aristogiton, hated Hippias and his family, so they plotted to murder the tyrant while he was at a public festival.

The two assassins waited until Hippias was surrounded by crowds of happy people before they moved in for the kill.

Hippias escaped their daggers, but his younger brother, Hipparchus, wasn't so lucky.

The murder of his brother and the attempt on his own life changed Hippias dramatically. He became obsessed by the idea that people were plotting against him.

Before long, anyone Hippias thought might be an enemy was arrested and executed.

INTENT ON MURDER: The two assassins pull out their daggers as Hippias approaches.

AND STAY OUT!

Life under Hippias became harsher and harsher, until finally the Athenians could bear it no longer. They asked for help from the nearby city-state of Sparta.

With the Spartan soldiers behind them, the people of Athens drove Hippias out of their city once and for all. The rule of the tyrants had been smashed.

The Athenians now took their government into their own hands.

Under the guidance of Clisthenes, a well-educated and wealthy Athenian, more and more power was given to the Assembly.

POWER TO THE PEOPLE

Now the Assembly was no longer just a place to meet and talk over the news of the day.

Instead, all free men of Athens gathered there to decide how the city was run — each man had a say and could vote on any decisions that had to be made. Athens was now a democracy.

And within no more than 20 years, the city had become famous as a rich and powerful state, governed by a strong Assembly.

Athens didn't need a single supreme ruler to lead it to power. The city chose to rely on its people, instead — a choice that paid off.

HOW IT ALL BEGAN

■ IN 499 B.C., Greeks who were living under Persian rule rebelled against the Persian king, Darius I. Darius harshly defeated the rebels and went on to invade Greece itself.

■ PERSIA was a superpower in those days, while Greece was just a collection of small city-states on Persia's western borders. Yet in 490 B.C., Athens beat the Persians in a heroic battle at Marathon, in southern Greece.

■ DARIUS died four years later, in 486 B.C., and his son Xerxes inherited the throne. Xerxes swore to take revenge on Greece for the humiliating defeat at Marathon. ■

GREECE IN PERIL

Illustrated by TUDOR HUMPHRIES

IN THE SPRING of 480 B.C., Greece faced the greatest threat it has ever known. The mighty Persian Empire, led by Xerxes, King of Kings, set out to crush our country once and for all.

A FORCE OF 200,000 soldiers was on its way to Greece, headed by the elite Persian troops, the famous "Immortals," and backed up by a vast fleet of Persian warships.

As the Persian army swept through northern Greece, it seemed that nothing and no one could bar its way.

A handful of brave Greek soldiers — mainly Spartans — tried to halt Xerxes and his army at Thermopylae. But after three days of fighting, the Persians burst through, swarming across central Greece like angry bees.

The city of Athens seemed certain to fall, and women and children were hurriedly shipped out of danger.

Only a few hundred men remained behind. Desperately they tried to defend the city — but they failed, and every single man died in the attempt.

Athens was burned to the ground. Even the

IN FLAMES: The temples of Athens are destroyed.

glorious temples on the Acropolis, the rocky hill at the very heart of the city, were destroyed.

XERXES CRUSHED

Then, in September, the tables were finally turned against Xerxes.

The angry Athenians regrouped under the brilliant leadership of Themistocles. Skillfully,

he tricked the Persian fleet into a battle near the island of Salamis, where he destroyed many of their warships.

Xerxes flew into a rage over this defeat and returned home. A year later, the troops he'd left behind were crushed at the Battle of Plataea.

The Persian menace had finally been driven from our lands, never to return. ■

OUR BRAVE BOYS

NO MATTER HOW long our history, our warriors' brave stand at Thermopylae will never be forgotten.

XERXES' soldiers were unable to cross the steep and treacherous mountains in central Greece. Instead, they had to travel along the narrow strip of coast at Thermopylae.

Although vastly out-numbered, a tiny force of southern Greeks set out to block their way.

THEY LAUGHED AT DEATH

Before the battle, our brave Greek soldiers were warned that "the flight of Persian arrows would block out the sun."

"Fine," replied the Spartan hero Dieneces. "We prefer to fight in the shade . . ."

Our courageous soldiers stood their ground and fought to the last man. Against all odds, they held back Xerxes' army for three whole days, killing thousands of his finest Persian troops. ■

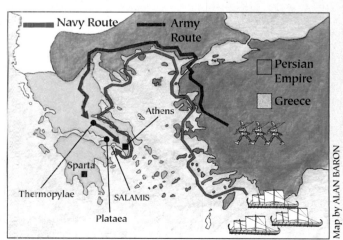

INVASION: The Persians' route into Greece by land and sea.

Map by ALAN BARON

SPARTA ATTACKS!

Illustrated by BOB MOULDER

ON THE MARCH: Thousands of Spartan soldiers advance on the city of Athens.

MOST OF GREECE was united in the war against Persia. But just 50 years later, Greek fought against Greek in a long and bitter conflict. Two of our most powerful city-states, Athens and Sparta, were at each other's throat.

SPARTA CLAIMED that Athens had become too rich and powerful—the city needed to be taught a lesson.

And who better to do it than Sparta, the city with the finest fighters in all of Greece.

The first attack came in 431 B.C. The horrified Athenians could hardly believe their eyes.

Beyond their high city walls rose a thick cloud of black smoke. Spartan troops, armor glinting in the sun, were setting fire to the nearby farms and chopping down the precious olive groves.

DOWN WITH ATHENS

DOWN WITH ATHENS

Cartoon by MARTIN BROWN

The Athenians were furious! They wanted to send out an army to drive the attackers away.

But the Athenian leader, Pericles, warned that this was just what Sparta *wanted* them to do.

With over 10,000 of the fiercest troops in Greece, the Spartans could easily defeat the Athenians—if only they could lure them out of the city to fight.

DEVASTATING RAID

Instead, said Pericles, Athens would rely on its strong navy, just as it had in the war with Persia.

So the Athenian ships launched a cunning raid on Spartan lands, and Athens was saved—for the moment.

The war dragged on for many long years, with Athens always avoiding an all-out battle. But in the end, the city made a crucial mistake.

THOUSANDS DEAD

In 415 B.C., Athens tried to add to its territory by conquering the island of Sicily. The results were disastrous—thousands of Athenian soldiers and hundreds of warships were lost.

The Spartans leaped on Athens's weakness and cut off the city's supply of wealth from its silver mines. Then Sparta built up a big fleet of its own, using the help of Persia, its old enemy.

Finally, in 405 B.C., the unthinkable happened. The new Spartan navy attacked and destroyed the Athenian fleet.

The Spartans now surrounded Athens at sea as well as on land, cutting off its food supplies. In 404 B.C., the starving Athenians finally surrendered.

Sparta was now the leading city in Greece—but other city-states were snapping at its heels.

While the old powers had been locked in combat, the world had moved on.

ALEXANDER WINS!

Illustrated by TUDOR HUMPHRIES

HORSE CITY!

Alexander has named a new Indian city Bucephala after his horse.

Alexander was 11 years old when he first got the horse Bucephalus — yet he was the *only* one who could tame it.

The horse soon became famous for carrying his master into battle, and now its name will go down in history.

HEROIC STAND: Greek soldiers face the terrifying might of Indian war elephants. n 326 B.C.

IN 334 B.C., A YOUNG MAN from Macedonia, in the far north of Greece, led an army into Asia, and changed our world forever. He was Alexander — the greatest ruler Greece has ever seen!

ALEXANDER was only 20 years old when he inherited his kingdom from his father. King Philip II had brought our whole country under Macedonian control, but few Greek cities would accept his young son as their new ruler.

Using a mixture of charm and savage threats, Alexander persuaded the city-states to accept his leadership. Then, in 334 B.C., he set his sights on greater things.

Alexander gathered together a united Greek army and led it into Persia. He traveled to Egypt and freed it from the Persians' rule. Then he fought his way across the Persian Empire, crushing its power forever.

The following year, Alexander and his army swept eastward through Asia, conquering all before them. By 326 B.C., they had fought their way to the fabled lands of India.

But Alexander's troops now faced a far more terrifying weapon than anything they had ever seen before — hundreds of Indian war elephants.

Our heroic soldiers fought the elephants and won, but homesick and weary of battle, they refused to go further.

Reluctantly, Alexander returned to Babylon and began making plans for a new empire.

DEATH OF A LEGEND

But, weakened by battle wounds, Alexander soon became ill with a fever. Tragically, on June 10, 323 B.C., this brilliant young leader died. He was only 32 years old.

After the death of Alexander, his vast empire crumbled and was split into separate kingdoms, ruled by his generals.

But one thing still unites these distant lands — our own Greek language and culture, the gift of Alexander and his army.

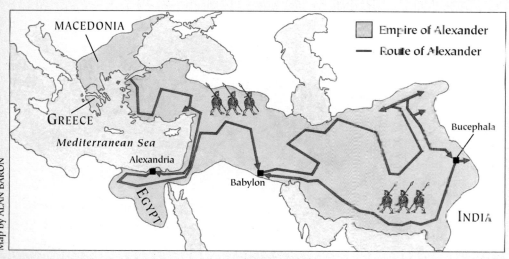

MACEDONIA

GREECE

Mediterranean Sea

Alexandria

EGYPT

Babylon

Bucephala

INDIA

☐ Empire of Alexander
— Route of Alexander

Map by ALAN BARON

ALEXANDER'S EMPIRE: At its height, it stretched across Persia all the way to India.

A PERFECT GREEK?

WE ALL KNOW the perfect Greek citizen. Or do we? To some, he's a fine speaker who can persuade people to do what he wants. To others, he's more likely to be a man of action and few words. Try *The Greek News's* quiz to see how *you* measure up.

1 A neighbor's slave has run away. *Do you:*
a) feel sorry for the slave and offer to hide him?
b) help your neighbor catch the slave and give him a good beating?
c) say that it's none of your business?

2 There's an important religious festival in your city. *Do you:*
a) join in and make expensive sacrifices to keep the gods happy?
b) complain that the money would be better spent on building new houses?
c) take the day off and go to the country?

3 War against your city could break out at any time. But your teenage son is lazy and won't attend weapons training. *Do you:*

a) tell him that fighting is a waste of time and that you would prefer him to enjoy himself?
b) force him to go and learn to fight like a man?
c) tell him to concentrate on making money in the family business instead?

4 Your main rival is a very powerful man, but you are sure he is cheating your state out of public money. *Do you:*
a) start a quarrel with him the next time you meet him in the street?
b) send your slaves around to his house to beat him up?
c) take him to the law court and demand that he be punished for his unlawful behavior?

Score one point for each correct answer.

■ **1b:** Our country could not survive without using slave labor, and it is in all our interests to capture runaways.

■ **2a:** Every Greek has to respect the gods and offer sacrifices to them. Otherwise the gods may become angry and punish the whole city.

■ **3b:** City-states need their citizens to protect them in times of trouble. All young men should train to fight.

■ **4c:** If our citizens quarrel, their city becomes easy for enemies to capture. Any disagreements should be settled in the law courts, where all citizens can vote on the rights and wrongs of the case.

HOW DID YOU SCORE?

0 You deserve to be captured by pirates and forced to sweat as a galley slave!

1–2 You tend to be selfish and should try harder to be a good citizen.

3 You are a credit to your city and deserve our praise.

4 You are a hero, and a far better citizen than most of our political leaders!

TABLE TALK

THIS ARTICLE, SENT in by an Athenian merchant, just goes to prove the old saying — we Greeks love nothing as much as politics!

WITH A GROUP of other merchants from Athens, I recently held a feast for some visiting Egyptian traders.

Our guests enjoyed the food, but when the conversation turned to politics, they raised their eyebrows.

YOU'RE SO BORING!

"You Greeks are *always* talking about politics," said one. "You're so boring! And what's more, all your cities seem to have different types of government!"

"Well," I replied, "it's really quite simple. There's monarchy, or rule by a king — actually, the Spartans have two kings.

Then, of course, there's aristocracy, or rule by noble families. And if one person seizes absolute power, we call it tyranny — rule by a tyrant.

Now, as you know, here in Athens we have democracy, rule by the people . . ."

"The people? You mean the *mob* more like!" one of my guests interrupted rudely.

Cartoon by MARTIN BROWN

A FATE WORSE THAN DEATH: A boring speaker is dragged away by the Assembly slaves.

"Oh, dear me, no!" I objected. "We are very particular about whom we allow to vote. No women, no slaves . . . only free men.

About 40,000 of us Athenians have the vote, you know, and as many as 6,000 of us may go to a really important Assembly meeting — that's where we all decide what action we should take.

The Assembly meets almost every week.

Before this, a special group of 500 men has already decided what we need to talk about.

SAY YOUR PIECE

Then any man who wants to can stand up and say what he thinks we should do, whether it's a change in the law, or a decision about going to war.

Of course, some of the speakers are a lot better than others. And sometimes we boo a bad speaker until he's dragged off! But in the end, we all get to raise our hands and vote for what we want to do. It's fun — and it's fair."

At that moment, loud snores made me realize that all of my Egyptian guests had fallen asleep.

Some people just have no appreciation of the really important things in life!

SPEAK UP AND SPEAK OUT!

Illustrated by RON TINER

FOR MOST young Athenians, that first speech to the Assembly can be a daunting experience. So turn the jeers to cheers, with *The Greek News's* guide to speaking up.

■ All the older men will be called to speak first. Keep cool while you're waiting, and plan what you're going to say.

■ If you don't belong to a powerful family, it's going to be harder to get people to listen to you, so talk about subjects you understand best. If you know about shipbuilding, for example, wait for a debate on the navy.

■ Ignore any booing and jeering. Don't forget that all free Athenian men (not slaves, of course) have the right to speak in the Assembly.

■ End your speech with a witty phrase to make people remember you.

■ Above all, don't give up. It's not often that the Assembly slaves drag off a boring speaker. And if you do have something to say, and can say it honestly and clearly, people will sit up and take notice.

INTO BATTLE

Illustrated by RON TINER

CROUCH AND DEFEND: Hoplites prepare for an enemy attack.

POETS AND POLITICIANS love to praise the incredible bravery and discipline of our Greek soldiers. But what is it *really* like to face the enemy in war? *The Greek News* hears from a battle-scarred survivor.

I WELL REMEMBER the pride I felt as I set off to my first battle, side by side with all the young men from our town.

My costly armor showed I was one of the famous foot soldiers, called hoplites, and that I came from a wealthy family. I was 18 years old, and of course I had been training for this moment ever since I was a young boy.

READY FOR A FIGHT

I started with boxing and wrestling lessons. Then, when I was older, weapons drill—all day under the blazing sun!

"At ease! Raise spear! Crouch and defend . . . "

On the day of a battle, I'd have a sick feeling of fear in my stomach. But it helped to have my friends beside me—we hoplites always trained in the same unit.

Then the war pipes would begin to play, and thousands of voices would chant the battle song. And we'd march straight toward the enemy ranks, shoulder to shoulder, shields raised —all of us ready to stab with our spears when the command was given.

Fighting? It's not the way they describe it in plays and poems, you know. It's messy and ugly! Steel on steel, the hissing flight of arrows, thudding shields, cries and groans, sweat, and agonizing pain.

Afterward, there's the terrible job of carrying our wounded away from the battlefield on their shields, and of burying dead friends. Then there's the weary march home.

WE WILL REMEMBER

Oh, we were welcomed back as heroes, and today we're all well respected in our towns. But I'll never forget my lost comrades, the ones who didn't have the chance to grow old. ◻

> I still remember the oath we all had to swear. It began:
> **"I shall fight all my days and be prepared to lay down my life for freedom."**

CHANGING FACE OF WAR

Would a soldier from the Persian wars recognize the way we fight today? We asked an experienced army commander . . .

■ The armor hasn't changed much. Leg plates are still made out of bronze, while breastplates are made of either bronze or stiff linen protected by small metal plates.

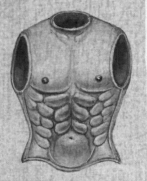

Bronze breastplate

■ A curved, slashing sword is more popular these days than the old-fashioned straight kind of sword.

Straight sword and curved sword

■ Back in the Persian wars, the hoplites were vital to our armies. Today, we make more use of archers and cavalry. We even fight from war elephants now, as warriors do in far-off India. ◻

SEA DOG TELLS ALL

Illustrated by BOB MOULDER

PERFECT POSITIONING: A trireme successfully rams an enemy ship

MANY A BATTLE has depended on triremes—they are the backbone of our navies. Here, a sea captain reveals the secrets of winning a fight at sea.

? Who is the most important person on board ship?

A clever captain is absolutely vital. He has to outthink the enemy and try to get his boat into the best position.

Then he can use the huge bronze spike that's just under the water at the front of his boat. He rams the enemy ship through its side, where the timbers are weakest.

Then, the captain just leaves the enemy ship to sink and its crew to drown.

? Do you always manage to ram the other ship?

Oh, no! Sometimes the triremes get jammed together.

This is when the whole ship relies upon its fighters — the archers to shoot arrows, and the soldiers to storm onto the enemy ship. The rowers can only hide behind a leather curtain.

? So getting the ship into the right position is what counts?

Absolutely! And don't forget that you've got 170 oarsmen in each ship, every one of them rowing with all of his might. Without the piper to mark the rhythm of their rowing, it would be chaos!

? Would you advise serving in a navy?

Certainly! All the men get paid a daily wage — they can earn as much as a skilled craftsman.

And, of course, they can take pride in serving in the finest navies in the world. ✕

TRIREMES: THE FACTS

Average speed:	6 miles per hour
Top speed:	9 miles per hour
Oar power:	3 rows each side
	31 oars in top row
	27 oars in each bottom row
	Total: 170 oars

Removable sails

Each oar: 14 feet long

Pointed bronze ram

Steering oar

Total length: 121 feet

Illustrated by PETER MORTER

THE LAND OF THE BRAVE

Illustrated by CHRISTIAN HOOK

TOUGH MEN, tough women, tough words, and tough food — that's the reputation of the Spartans. But how much does the rest of Greece really know about this secretive society? We sent our travel writer to investigate.

WE ALL KNOW that the Spartans are the best fighters in Greece.

So you can imagine my mixed feelings as I made my way toward this southern kingdom. What would I find?

Well, the place is pleasant enough, but the food is absolutely disgusting. And as for the people — they're as hard as nails!

Of course, fighting is important to all Greek citizens, but in Sparta the whole society is obsessed with war!

At just 7 years old, boys are sent away from their mothers to live in special training camps.

They're kept cold and hungry, and forced to go barefoot. They have to learn to bear pain and obey all orders without question.

Spartan boys aren't punished for stealing, I was told. Instead, they're punished for being foolish enough to get caught!

And even as grown men, they still have to live in barracks, away from their wife and their children.

But despite all this, not everyone grows up to be a hero. And there

is a particularly harsh punishment for cowards in Sparta.

A coward is called a Trembler and is forced to wear silly clothes. He's even made to grow a mustache on just one side of his face.

Anyone can hit a Trembler, whenever they feel like it.

GIRL POWER

As for girls — in Sparta they're trained to run and jump, and even to wrestle.

And they strip off all their clothes when they do athletics, just like the men! Can you imagine girls from any other Greek city doing something like that? Most of them would be horrified just at the thought.

But Spartans believe that if a man's duty is to fight, a woman's is to bear children. So they make their girls strong for childbirth, just as they train their boys for war.

Pain, cold, hunger, suffering — that's what life in Sparta is about. The people of this kingdom really do believe that the good things in life make you lazy and a coward.

My advice to you is — don't go there unless you have to!

SPARTAN PRIDE: A warrior wears the famous red cloak of courage.

WE'RE TOUGH!

GRRRR

Cartoon by MARTIN BROWN

OUR WAYS WIN WARS

Illustrated by NICKY COONEY

THERE ARE TWO SIDES to every story, so *The Greek News* spoke to a Spartan to find out what *he* had to say about his homeland.

YOUR TRAVEL writer sneers at our customs and insults our women. Well, let him! We won't change our ways.

It's obvious that the rest of Greece is jealous of our bravery.

Just look at the famous struggle at Thermopylae. There's a story about that battle, you know.

The Persian troops were scouting around, spying on our front line. But did they find our soldiers worrying about the upcoming battle?

No! Our men were chatting and combing out their long hair, cool as cucumbers. Now *that* takes real courage!

LIFE IS HARSH

And why is refusing to pamper our children such a bad thing? Life is painful, and the earlier we all get used to it the better.

Do you know how we teach our boys bravery? Cheese is placed on the altar of the goddess Orthia, and hungry boys are whipped as they run to grab it. The boy who gets the most is the one who can put up with the heaviest whipping.

And there's no doubt about it—our methods work. Everyone knows that Spartan boys grow into the fiercest fighters in all of Greece.

That's why we don't need a stone wall to protect our city. We have something far stronger to defend us—all the brave men, women, and children of Sparta!

TRIAL OF STRENGTH: Spartan boys undergo a test of bravery.

RISE AND FALL

◆

■ Sparta first became a powerful city-state in about 600 B.C. This was when it conquered the land near it and forced the people who lived there into slavery.

■ Citizens of Sparta have little say in how their state is run—there's no democracy. Sparta is ruled by not one king, but two.

■ In 431 B.C., Sparta began a long war with Athens. Sparta won in 404 B.C., and became the most powerful city-state in all of Greece.

■ But in 369 B.C., the city of Thebes captured most of Sparta's land. Sparta survived, but its strength had been broken at last.

A LAND APART

THESE OLD PUBLIC NOTICES show how Sparta has always been a very unusual state.

COWARDICE

has no place in Sparta! For falling ill before the Battle of Thermopylae, Aristodamus is now a Trembler. He is a disgrace to us all. Let no man marry his sisters or his daughters.

RUNAWAY SLAVES

Two male slaves last seen heading for the mountains. Don't bring them back alive — slaughter them on sight!

A RESPECTED SPARTAN CITIZEN

has been injured and can no longer have children of his own. His wife is still able to bear more children for Sparta. The couple seeks a healthy citizen willing to father children.

✳

Apply in person to the kings.

Map labels:

- **TIN** *from Britain*
- **IRON** *from Elba*
- **SLAVES** *from eastern Europe*
- **GRAIN** *from the Black Sea coast*
- EUROPE
- **TIMBER** *from the Black Sea coast*
- **FISH** *from the Black Sea*
- **SILVER** *from Spain*
- **GOLD** *from Turkey*
- **GREECE**
- *Mediterranean Sea*
- **COPPER** *from Cyprus*
- **CARPETS AND CUSHIONS** *from Tunisia*
- **PAPYRUS** *from Egypt*
- NORTH AFRICA
- **IVORY** *from Libya*

NOTHING BUT THE BEST!

Map by PETER MORTER

THERE'S NO DOUBT about it— Greek goods are the best in the world. So why are our markets flooded with so much foreign produce?

WELL, FOR ONE thing, we Greeks are very fond of the luxuries in life.

We love rich foods, like the almonds and dates we buy from Asia. Then there are exotic Asian perfumes, not to mention the wonderful carpets we import from Africa. Also, many of our craftworkers rely on foreign goods — some of our most beautiful jewelry is made from Spanish silver.

And where would our shipbuilders be without the timber we buy from other lands?

But more important than all of these is the basic foodstuff we have to bring into Greece.

Crops are difficult to grow in our rocky, dry homeland. Without the extra grain we get from the Black Sea region, we'd starve!

So there are many reasons why we need these goods from foreign lands. And it's fortunate for us that our own products are so popular abroad — because the money we make from selling our goods pays for those that we import.

Everyone knows our wines and olive oil are the best in the world — they're shipped out to every corner of the Mediterranean Sea.

And our fine pottery and metalwork is even bought by the barbarians in far-off Britain!

We can be proud that our goods sell so well abroad. It allows us to buy only the best for ourselves in return. Nothing else is good enough!

SLAVE TRADE

Illustrated by RON TINER

MAKE MONEY FAST: Slaves from all lands sell well in our markets.

SO YOU WANT TO make a quick profit? What about the slave trade? *The Greek News* gives you the arguments for and against.

FIRST OF ALL, you'll be doing your country a favor. How would we manage without slaves? Who'd do all the dirty work for us?

YOU CAN'T LOSE

And slaves are always in demand, so it's unlikely you'll lose your money. Wealthy families may need 50 or more slaves per household, and even the poorest farmers will need one or two.

If you find you can't place all your slaves with families, you can always sell some to the silver mines.

Unlike household slaves, who are often treated with too much kindness miners are quickly worn out by hard labor. And that means replacements are always needed— which means more business for you!

There's no trade without its problems, of course. Slaves are always running away

and have to be re-captured and branded.

You'll also have to pay for transporting your slaves, and for feeding them until they're sold.

But you won't find it difficult to get ahold of healthy new slaves. A steady supply is always being imported from abroad.

And in times of war, the market is flooded with captives of all kinds. Watch out for Greek slaves, they always fetch the highest prices!

Our advice is — if you have money to spare, spend it in the slave trade.

SLAVES
*from around the
Black Sea coast*

A S I A

PERFUMES
from Syria

SAFE MONEY!

Since every Greek city makes its own coins, how do you know which ones to trust? Here's *The Greek News*'s guide to the coins that we think are worth their weight.

Silver owl coin from Athens

Gold Pegasus coin from Lampsacus

Silver bee coin from Ephesus

Silver amphora coin from Thebes

Gold Apollo coin from Macedonia

Silver bull coin from the Italian colony of Thurii

SLAVE SALE, AT PRIENE

As a guide to prices, remember that a craftworker can earn one or two drachmas a day.

- Healthy little boy, train him yourself, 80 drachmas
- Young Greek woman, good at weaving, 160 drachmas
- Man, about 30, useful for heavy labor, 180 drachmas
- Man, 35, skilled vase painter, 270 drachmas

OLYMPIC GAMES SPOILED

Illustrated by ALAN LANGFORD

DISASTER STRIKES: Did a cheat tamper with this chariot before the race?

THE OLYMPIC GAMES are meant to be a religious celebration, yet all too often they are spoiled by cheating. *The Greek News* **takes a hard look at the facts.**

EVERY FOUR YEARS, at the famous contest at Olympia, there's the opportunity for Greeks to show their respect for Zeus, as the most powerful god of all.

GAMES STOP WARS

We even refuse to fight battles at this time so that thousands of men can come to the Games. Some even travel from Greek colonies as far away as the Black Sea, Egypt, and Spain.

But the festival is increasingly being spoiled by ugly scenes. Just look at all the penalty statues of Zeus around Olympia. Each of these statues was paid for by a cheat who was caught.

Critics say rewards for the winners are just too big. The prizes given at the Games themselves may be small—a simple wreath of olive leaves—but back at home the winning athletes are treated like superstars.

Their city gives them money, and people lavish gifts and the best food and drink on them. No wonder so many of the athletes want to win at any cost.

But athletes should remember that the aim of the Games is to encourage our men to maintain themselves at the peak of fitness for battle.

Surely winning is not so important. If our men are strong and can defend us, every Greek will be a winner!

Report from Olympia, 396 B.C.

WOMAN WINS!

Women are forbidden to enter the Olympics—on pain of death. But this year the winning team of horses at a chariot race was owned by a woman— Cynisca of Sparta.

Illustrated by JOHN TE BROCO

GUIDE TO EVENTS

Illustrated by NICKY COONEY

■ FOOTRACES

The main race, the sprint, covers almost 200 meters, and the winner becomes famous throughout the whole of Greece. The other footraces can be up to 3 miles in length.

Cheating: Cutting in front of other runners, tripping them, or elbowing them to one side.

■ CHARIOT RACING

Whether for two or four horses, these races are exciting and terrifying to watch. With so many horses and chariots thundering around the track, there is always the chance of a crash, and sometimes drivers get killed — brave men, since it's the owners who get the prize!

Cheating: Cutting in front of a rival chariot, especially on a curve. Sources close to The Greek News claim that rivals may tamper with a chariot before the race to make it fall apart.

■ BOXING

Each pair of fighters has to stand up to a battering, as well as to cuts made by the thick leather thongs wrapped tightly around their fists.

Cheating: Any blow to the lower belly or groin. Also, tripping an opponent, then hitting him when he stumbles and falls.

■ HORSERACING

This is one of the most dangerous sports. The ground is so rutted and rough from the chariot races that the riders risk being thrown and killed.

Cheating: The racehorses must be carefully guarded to make sure they aren't injured by opponents before the race begins.

■ RACING IN ARMOR

All-around strength is needed to be able to sprint while carrying a shield and wearing the heavy metal helmet of a hoplite soldier.

Cheating: Look out for contestants using their shields to barge into the other runners, making them trip.

■ WRESTLING

A fascinating contest. Pairs of men wrestle and batter each other until one gives up or is too badly injured to continue.

Cheating: Gouging of the opponent's eyes with the thumb, especially when his head is turned away from the umpire. Biting is another common practice.

■ JAVELIN & DISCUS

A skillful event, as the athlete has to find the best throwing angle and know exactly when to let go of the javelin or discus.

Cheating: The only way is to step over the mark when throwing.

■ LONG JUMP

Great concentration is needed to jump while swinging the hand-held weights that give the body an extra push.

Cheating: Watch out for a sly athlete sprawling forward as he lands, to confuse the umpire.

FULL STRETCH: A javelin thrower, discus thrower, and long jumper go through their paces.

WOMEN TALK

A WOMAN'S PLACE is at the loom. Or is it? *The Greek News* talks to two women with very different views.

The first is a woman from Rhodes, who has been married for ten years.

❓ Are you happy in your marriage?
Well, I do get a bit fed up sometimes. My whole life seems to be spent running the household — giving orders to the slaves or looking after the children.

I *do* envy my husband. He's often out working, or wining and dining. I can't do those things!

I never see anyone really. I have to stay in the women's quarters all of the time. When my husband has friends over for dinner, I'm not allowed to join them.

❓ But you do get out of the house sometimes?
Only a few times a year, for religious festivals.

❓ But isn't running a home enough to keep any woman busy?
Women can do more than men think! There *are* women who manage jobs outside the home. Some work as market traders, while others help deliver babies. There have also been famous women poets, like Sappho.

❓ Do you think women should have more say in what goes on?
Well, men obviously don't think so! After all, we can't make speeches in the Assembly, or vote on any decisions they make there. I think they forget that some Greek cities have had women rulers.

❓ Any last advice to young women?
Enjoy your girlhood — once you're married there'll be nothing but housework and children!

HOUSEWORK: Running a household is a full-time job.

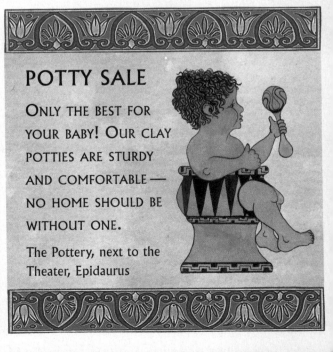

BACK

The second woman we interviewed had a rather different outlook on life. She is a 14-year-old girl from Thebes, who is about to marry a wealthy 30-year-old man.

? Are you very excited about your wedding?

Of course, I am! I have been ever since my father arranged it four years ago.

A girl's wedding is the most important day in her life. I can't wait to offer up my childhood toys to the goddess Artemis, the protector of all young women.

I shall wear my finest linen and jewelry for the celebration—there will be music and songs, and feasting.

I'm looking forward to seeing my husband for the first time, too. So far, only my father has met him. All I know is that he comes from a good family.

? What do you want from your marriage?

Peace of mind, I suppose. My husband will make all the decisions and look after me. And being married will allow me to start my real life, as a wife and a mother.

I intend to serve my husband well and to run his household smoothly. I'll keep myself busy weaving beautiful cloth, and making sure that all the meals are wonderful.

And I'd like to have babies, of course.

? Would you rather have a boy or a girl?

Oh, a boy! Everyone wants a boy who'll grow up to serve his country, and bring wealth and fame to his family.

But if the gods give me a girl, so be it. I'll teach her to be a good wife when *she* grows up.

? Do you have any fears about your life?

Well, I *am* scared of childbirth—it's dangerous and so many women die!

But I still want as many babies as I can have. Then there will be plenty of children to look after my husband and me when we grow old.

THE BIG NIGHT: The groom takes his bride from her home to begin her married life.

Illustrated by RON TINER

WHICH GOD?

ZEUS
The chief of all the gods, and god of the sky, storms, the wind, the family, and friendship. He punishes the wicked with thunderbolts.

HERA
The wife of Zeus, queen of the sky, goddess of all women, of marriage, and of mothers. Her sacred animal is the cow.

ATHENA
The goddess of cities, war, and wisdom. Protector of spinners, weavers, and all skilled workers. Her symbol is the owl.

APOLLO
The god of sunlight, colonies, crops, and music. Also the god of prophecy, honored at Delphi. His symbol is the lyre.

PLEASING

Illustrated by BARBARA LOFTHOUSE

You KNOW WHAT it's like. One minute your life is going smoothly, then, just when you least expect it, the gods turn their back on you and disaster strikes! Don't panic—*The Greek News* will tell you everything you need to know about keeping the gods on your side.

PERHAPS YOU'VE broken a vow to one of the gods? Or maybe a particular god or goddess has helped you and you've ignored his or her aid?

Remember, each of the gods looks after different parts of our lives. So, if Asclepius, the god of medicine, has cured you of a terrible illness, you're in his debt. Or if the sea god, Poseidon, has saved you from a shipwreck, you need to thank him.

Repaying a god can be expensive, though. You'll have to travel to the god's temple, and pay for an animal to be sacrificed.

Make sure the animal is one the god favors. Some gods are choosy—Zeus, for example, will only accept oxen.

But your money will be well spent—a sacrifice always pleases the gods.

In fact, if you have a problem and need a god's help, then a sacrifice is the best way to win it.

The trouble is, we have so many gods! How do you know which one to turn to? Often, it's quickest just to go straight to the top and ask the help of a major god.

Even then, you still have to decide which is the best god for you. And although everyone knows who the major gods are, it's easy to forget all

ORACLE SPEAKS OUT!

Illustrated by ANGUS McBRIDE

EVERY SPRING, Greeks and foreigners alike travel to the oracle in the mountains at Delphi. But what is it really like to visit this strange priestess, and why *do* people come from so far away? *The Greek News* sent a reporter to find out.

HOLY MESSENGER: A priest waits for the oracle's words.

"SHOULD I GO to war?" asked an eastern prince.

"Should I marry my neighbor's daughter?" asked a worried young man from Thrace.

Our questions may have been different, but we had all come to the famous oracle at Delphi for the same thing—a glimpse into the future, to help make a decision.

Inside the temple, thick clouds of mist were billowing up from deep below the ground.

WORDS FROM THE GOD

The oracle groaned and mumbled in a trance, and a priest strained to catch her words. Or rather the words of the god, for it

THE GODS

WHICH GOD?

the different areas they protect. So you might find the Which God? guide on these pages a help when deciding.

OX: Zeus's chosen sacrifice.

However, sacrificing to the gods isn't just about repaying debts or solving problems. It's also wise to honor the god or goddess who protects your city. After all, if your city is attacked, everyone will suffer, including you!

Of course, the best way to please the gods is to join a temple. As a priest or priestess, you will take care of the building, its statues, and its treasures. You will also be responsible for sacrifices.

But do take time to think carefully before you make up your mind to take this step. Temple life doesn't suit everyone.

Whatever you decide, never forget that the gods rule every part of our lives. We ignore them at our peril!

was really the great Apollo himself who was speaking through the oracle's mouth.

We had each given treasure to the temple in payment for our question. Eagerly we listened in turn to the god's reply.

But it must be said that many of the pilgrims looked even *more* puzzled afterward than they had before!

The oracle rarely answers a question directly, and the god's words often have more than one meaning.

A good example of this is the fate that

befell King Croesus of Lydia back in 546 B.C. The oracle told him that if he attacked Persia, a great empire would fall. So the king did attack — but the empire that fell was his own!

As we climbed back down from Delphi to the coast, I reminded my fellow pilgrims of the tragic story of King Croesus.

And we all agreed that we would need to think very carefully indeed about our own message from the god Apollo.

But there was one thing we *were* certain of — a glimpse into the future was worth any price!

GREATEST OF THE GODS: At 43 feet high, the awesome statue of Zeus at Olympia towers above his worshippers.

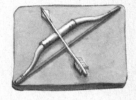

ARTEMIS
The huntress with her bow and arrow. Goddess of wild animals, purity, and birth. A favorite with country people.

POSEIDON
The god of the sea and all water, armed with his hunting trident. Bringer of earthquakes.

APHRODITE
The goddess of love, beauty, fertility, and nature. Her symbol is the dove.

DIONYSUS
The god of wine and grapes, and also of pleasure. His symbol is the drinking cup.

MORE SCHOOL?

Illustrated by ANDREW WHEATCROFT

WASTED EFFORT? Should boys be in school, or learning their father's trade?

PEOPLE THINK OF Greece as a center of great learning. Yet most of our children can't even read and write! *The Greek News* asked *you*, the readers, if more boys should be sent to school.

■ AGAINST SCHOOL

Frankly, most of you thought education was a waste of time and money. The following examples give a pretty clear idea of your replies:

"Only rich families can afford to send their sons to school or to buy a well-educated slave to teach them. How many of us have the money to do that sort of thing?"

"What use is school in later life? A boy should be learning about his father's trade, whether it's farming, mending shoes, or making pottery."

"It's crazy to send a boy off to school at 7 years old. That's just when he's starting to be useful around the farm or in the workshop."

■ FOR SCHOOL

It was only the wealthiest among you who had anything good to say about education. The following view was typical:

"Education sets our sons apart from the common people.

And they need to go to school until they are 18 years old. It takes at least seven or eight years just to beat some basic learning into them — reading, writing, math, music, athletics, that sort of thing.

Only when a boy is 15 or 16 years old is he ready to be taught some of the higher arts, such as learning how to speak cleverly in public. With this skill, he can help his family gain more power in the Assembly.

Mind you, there's not much point in educating every boy. Reading and writing's not much use on the farm, now, is it!"

So, as with so many things in life, it all seems to depend on how much money you have. ▨

GIRLS, TOO?

SHOULD GIRLS be taught to read and write? What did *you*, the public, think?

"OH, NO," seemed to be the answer, "most definitely not!"

Many of you felt there was no point in educating girls. They need to learn things like spinning, weaving, and cooking, in order to run a household smoothly once they are married. And the best place to learn these skills is at home with their mother!

A few rich parents said they would let their daughters learn to read, but only from a slave at home — never by going out to school. ▨

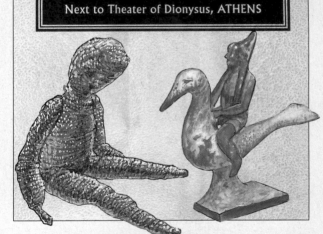

BEHIND THE SCENES

Illustrated by BARBARA LOFTHOUSE

ACTORS sweat for hours under heavy masks, pretending to be anything from gods to frogs — what a strange way to earn a living! We spent a night at the theater and asked one of the leading actors to take us behind the scenes . . .

CCMEDY IN ACTION: A silly-looking lover, with the help of his slave, woos a maiden.

❓ Why *do* actors wear masks?

It's all part of the mystery. We actors are ordinary men, but our masks can change us into runaway slaves, ugly monsters, or even beautiful women.

❓ What other tricks do you use?

Oh, plenty. I can't tell you them all because that would destroy the magic!

But one of the most obvious is the painted panels used to change the scenery in a play from a temple, say, to a forest.

Another very clever effect is when the gods appear in the sky at the end of the great tragedy plays. We use a lifting machine to make the actors fly.

❓ What's it like being up on stage?

Well, I was really scared the first time I performed on the main stage. Especially since there are never more than three actors up there at one time.

It's not so bad down on the theater floor, where the chorus actors stand. There are usually about 12 chorus actors making comments to the audience about what's happening in the play. But in some plays there can be as many as 50.

❓ Why don't women act in plays?

Well, what man would want his daughter or his wife up on a stage being stared at — even if she was wearing a mask? It would be a disgrace!

❓ Which plays do you prefer — comedies or tragedies?

Well, I love the tragedies. They have everything — lots of action and great stories about heroes and villains from long ago.

But my favorite plays are comedies, especially those by the great writer Aristophanes. Comedies poke fun at silly or pompous leaders and politicians. And being laughed at in a play can sometimes make these people change the way they behave.

❓ Could you ever give up the theater?

Oh, no, never! I love the applause too much. ⊠

PRIDE OF ATHENS

Illustrated by ALAN BARON and GEORGE THOMPSON

This most spectacular temple is made of local marble. There are no less than 8 columns across the front of the building, and 17 on each side.

Painted stone carvings decorate the walls inside and outside. They show dramatic scenes from legends, wars, and the great processions held in honor of Athena.

Inside the temple is the sacred chamber of the goddess herself. Here the vast statue of Athena, glinting with gold, towers up into the roof.

Behind her is the treasury, a room packed with the spoils of war — gold and silver cups, helmets, and shields.

But we should never forget that this entire building is a treasure — and not just for Athens, for the whole world.

THE PARTHENON: A glorious temple to Athena.

WHO HAS NOT HEARD of the Parthenon in Athens — surely one of the world's finest buildings.

ATHENIANS ARE quite right to be proud of their huge temple to the goddess Athena, high on the hill of the Acropolis.

This glorious building marks Athens's recovery from the destruction of the Persian wars.

The unholy Persians had burned the old half-finished temple to the ground. So the Athenians resolved to build a bigger temple on the same site.

Work began in 447 B.C., and in 14 years the new building was finished.

GOLDEN GLORY: Athena's statue is almost 43 feet high.

How much did the Parthenon cost Athens?

For the temple:
- quarrying the stone
- carting the stone
- shaping the stone
- assembling the floor, walls, and columns
- making the doors
- tiling the roof in marble
- carving statues

- painting statues
- architect's fee
- sculptors' fees
- laborers' wages

Cost: nearly 3 million drachmas

At the time of building the Parthenon, a skilled worker could earn up to one drachma a day.

For Athena's statue:
- wood for the core
- ivory for the skin
- gold for the armor
- hoisting the statue into place
- sculptor's fee
- laborers' wages

Cost: about 3.5 million drachmas

LIVING IN A PIGSTY

So MANY OF OUR CITIES are crowded and smelly. *The Greek News* talks to a top architect to find out why this is so.

❓ What's wrong with our cities?

Well, one of the biggest problems is housing. Most homes start off with just one or two rooms — there really isn't enough space for people to raise families in them.

❓ How does this affect our cities?

People create extra space by adding more rooms in a haphazard way. It's a complete shambles! What we need to do is build larger houses in the first place.

❓ Is that all we need?

No, we also need to make the streets broader and straighter so there are no twisting alleys where robbers can hide.

And we should put in proper drains as well. You know how bad our cities smell in summer. People just throw their dirty water out into the street — and it's not *just* water! It has to stop.

We could also use more public fountains and tanks for collecting fresh rainwater.

❓ Do you think you'll ever be able to create such a city?

Well, all things are possible, but nobody wants to pay for these kinds of boring, everyday improvements.

They would rather be known for funding a grand and expensive temple, instead.

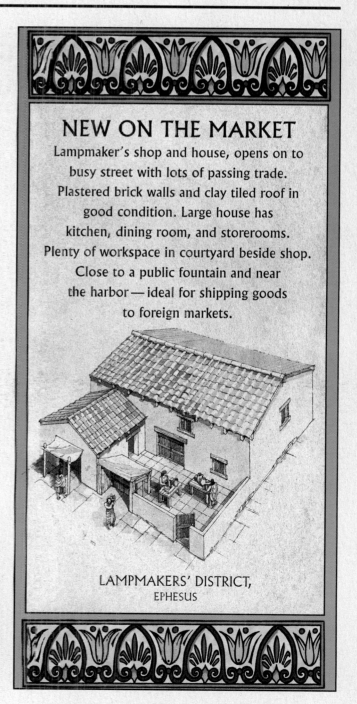

YOUR LIFE IN THEIR HANDS

Illustrated by ANGUS M^cBRIDE

EACH HEALER you talk to seems to have a different remedy, and each thinks *his* cure is the best! But what it all comes down to is a simple choice — the gods or nature.

MANY HEALERS believe that the gods *make* us ill, either as a punishment for our wickedness or pride, or because we haven't been honoring the gods enough.

When a woman dies in childbirth, for example, these healers say that she must have angered Artemis, the goddess of birth.

They will give you lucky charms to cure your sickness or to guard you against becoming ill. If that fails, they will send

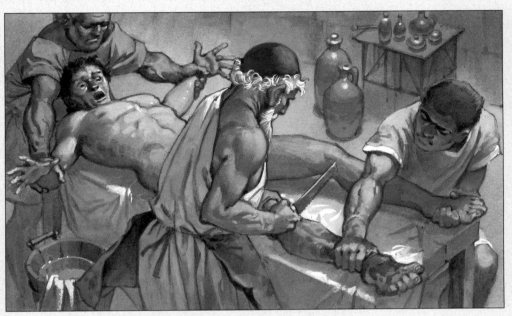

FATAL CHOICE: A healer prepares to operate. Would you rather put your trust in the gods?

you off to the shrine of the god Asclepius, who watches over all those who are sick and in pain.

So, if you also put your trust in the gods, then these healers are the right ones to choose.

But there are other healers — the people who follow the teachings of the famous Hippocrates.

This great man lived on the island of Cos in the 400s B.C. And his followers believe that most illnesses have natural causes.

They try to figure out why you're ill by studying everything about you — your breathing, what you eat, the water you drink, even where you live.

Then they might treat you with leeches, to suck out any harmful poisons in your blood.

They might give you medicine made from powerful herbs, or even remove part of your body, if necessary.

Or, you might just be told to exercise more or eat different foods.

But whatever their remedy, these healers will do their best to cure you. They even take an oath, promising to treat their patients well! ▣

MIRACLE CURES

Illustrated by BARBARA LOFTHOUSE

OUR REPORTER went to Epidaurus to join those in search of a cure at the holiest temple of Asclepius.

THE WEARY pilgrims I joined on the way to Epidaurus had no doubts. The gods had made them ill and the god Asclepius would cure them.

Many had traveled for weeks to spend the night in the temple's sleeping quarters. If the pilgrims are lucky, the god will visit

them in their dreams. This vision alone may be enough to cure some people. Others are told by the god what treatment is best.

The night I spent at the temple was endless. I was woken time and again by people groaning in their sleep.

CLAY OFFERINGS: Left for the god, in thanks.

But by the morning, many of the patients were sleeping peacefully, their fevers gone. Others were sacrificing roosters in thanks to Asclepius.

And on my way out I noticed hundreds of offerings to the god, left by the grateful pilgrims. Many were clay models in the shape of hands, arms, legs, eyes, ears, or some other part of the body that the god had miraculously healed.

These lucky patients definitely believed they had plenty to thank Asclepius for. ▣

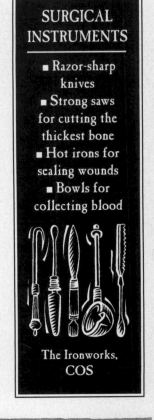

THE TRIAL OF Socrates, the great philosopher, took place in Athens today. Our reporter was at the scene when his sentence was passed . . .

In 399 B.C., *The Greek News* reported the dramatic end to the career of one of our greatest thinkers.

DEATH BY POISON!

Illustrated by CHRISTIAN HOOK

SOCRATES IS TO DIE! The jury of 501 men has made its decision— Socrates *is* guilty of not believing in the state-approved gods and of leading young people astray with his teaching.

Although he could still flee from Athens, Socrates has bravely, or perhaps foolishly, decided to kill himself by drinking the juice of the deadly hemlock plant.

Socrates, now in his seventies, has always been interested in study. In his youth, he gave up his business affairs for the world of ideas.

He became famous for his popular public discussions, where he would question someone without mercy until he had forced that person to think for himself.

Socrates' aim was to make people examine everything. And in the end, Athens's leaders felt that he had become a danger to the state.

Other thinkers have been seen as a threat to their government. But none has ever been silenced by death.

BITTER END: Socrates prepares to drink a cup of deadly hemlock juice.

IDEAS DON'T DIE!

OF COURSE, SOCRATES was not our country's only great thinker. There have been many brilliant scholars throughout our history. *The Greek News* looks back at a few of these great men of ideas.

■ **THALES**
Born in Miletus before 600 B.C., Thales was one of the first of our people to ask whether the gods were really responsible for things like floods and thunderstorms. Instead, he looked for the causes in nature.

■ **PLATO**
Plato was an Athenian, born around 429 B.C. He was a follower of Socrates and, like his hero, he became a philosopher.

Plato used Socrates' teachings to develop new ideas about running city-states and ruling people.

■ **ARISTOTLE**
Born near Macedonia in 384 B.C., Aristotle studied under Plato at his famous school in Athens. After this, he became tutor to a Macedonian prince —the young Alexander the Great.

Aristotle believed in looking carefully at all things to find out how they work.

He studied everything under the sun, from animals that live in the sea to how different Greek cities organize themselves.

FIRST FEAST!

Illustrated by RICHARD BERRIDGE

IT'S YOUR LUCKY night — you've been invited to your first grand feast. But how should you behave once you get there? *The Greek News* guides you through the perils of the highlife.

PARTY TIME: Food, wine, and acrobats — all the right ingredients for a great feast.

STEP 1
The big night arrives and you're there in your best clothes. Try to be patient while your host pours an offering of wine to the gods, and don't spoil it all by looking too hungry.

STEP 2
You've found heaven! There you are, draped with garlands and lying on soft cushions, while slaves bring you endless drinks of snow-chilled wine. You're feasting on succulent tuna fish, fresh local octopus, roast wild boar, and deer. Later on, there will be figs, pastries flavored with sweet wine, and honey cakes.

But don't get carried away. Try to look as if you dine like this every night in your own home.

STEP 3
Don't get drunk too early. Enjoy the music and watch the acrobats and dancing girls, but keep your wits about you. Go for the watered wine.

STEP 4
Later in the evening, the clever conversation turns to stupid jokes. And then people start to play silly games, like throwing their wine dregs at a target.

Watch out — you still need to be on your best behavior. You want to be invited back again!

So make sure you go home early, before you get too drunk and have to be carried home by your host's slaves. ◩

TREAT YOUR TASTE BUDS

OF COURSE, MOST of us won't ever get to a feast. Don't despair! *The Greek News* has some hints for making everyday meals more tasty.

BREAKFAST
Don't start the day on an empty stomach. Barley cake is filling — or make your barley porridge more interesting with myrtle berries, figs, or sun-dried grapes.

LUNCH
Keep it light. Liven up your bread and goat cheese with boiled eggs and salted or smoked fish. And, if you can afford it, try wheat bread instead of barley loaves.

EVENING MEAL
You will want something a bit special. Pigeon, chicken, and sausage are all cheap. Even if you can only afford lentils, chickpeas, or beans, add a few leeks or onions when they're in season, along with plenty of fresh mountain herbs.

If you're the hunting type, then try trapping hedgehogs, thrushes, or hares. They all make a good stew.

Finish with pears or pomegranates for a touch of sweetness. And wash it all down with barley water or diluted wine. ◩

GROW YOUR OWN

Illustrated by CHRISTIAN HOOK

OVER THE YEARS, we've answered hundreds of questions about every possible farming problem. So if you've just bought some land and don't know where to start — read on.

❓ Which grain crops should I grow?

If you have good rich soil, you can grow wheat — it always sells well.

But if you have the usual thin and rocky Greek soil, try growing barley instead. It's a tough, hardy crop.

Keep in mind that it can be risky growing either crop. A dry summer can spell disaster, while an early winter storm could flatten your harvest.

❓ My land is very hilly — how can I improve it?

The best way is to build low stone walls along the slopes, and pile earth against them to make terraces. It's hard work, but worth it, as the walls will stop the soil from being blown off by the wind, or washed away by winter rains.

❓ Are olives a good crop to choose?

Olives grow well nearly everywhere in Greece, and the oil always brings a good price.

But they're a long-term investment — trees take 40 years to reach their peak. And they're at risk in times of war. If enemy soldiers chop them down, you'll lose a lifetime's work in an instant!

❓ What about grapes?

They're another crop that grows well. But you'll need plenty of help at harvest time to pick the grapes and tread them into juice for wine.

PIPING UP: Music makes a grapetreader's task easier.

❓ And what are the best animals to raise?

There's always room for chickens in a farmyard, and you'll need donkeys and oxen, of course, to help with carrying loads and the plowing.

Cattle will make you money, but they do need lush grassland. Sheep and goats, on the other hand, can wander in the hills. But you must have a shepherd to keep away wolves and thieves. ◪

LOOK YOUR BEST

Illustrated by SUE SHIELDS

THE GREEK NEWS's top fashion tips have always kept you right up-to-date and looking good! Here's a selection of those styles that have proved to be classics over the years.

■ LADIES

By far the most elegant tunic is the long-sleeved chiton, made of the finest Egyptian linen, fastened along the arms, and belted at the waist into graceful folds.

But the old sleeveless tunic has proved to be a timeless favorite. It's so easy to wear — you just pin it at the shoulder. And you can spin the wool for it at home.

Everyone notices a carefully crafted piece of jewelry. So it's worth saving up for a few expensive gold or silver pieces. They can make the world of difference to a simple tunic.

For an unusual effect, choose a hairpin carved into a leaf or a flower, or a bracelet made in the shape of a snake.

■ GENTLEMEN

All men wear the same basic tunic, of course, but do keep yours long, at least to the knee. A short tunic is worn only by laborers, who have to make sure it doesn't get in the way when working.

For a truly stylish look, wrap your cloak around your body and drape one end of it casually over your shoulder.

Although the fashion for beards and long hair has gone a little out of style in recent years, many people still think that it looks manly. And long hair can be tied back neatly with a clasp if it gets in the way.

TOUCH OF CLASS

■ LADIES — your skin should be as pale as possible to set you apart from women who work outdoors all day. If you need to, lighten your skin with white powder.

■ GENTLEMEN — aim for a light tan so you don't look like a craftworker who stays indoors. But be careful! Too dark, and you'll be mistaken for a farm slave.

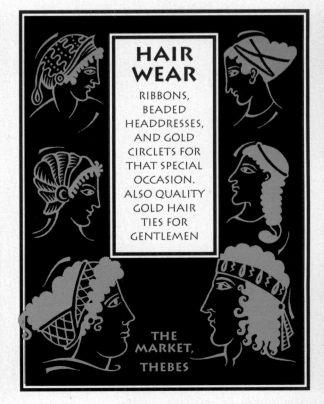

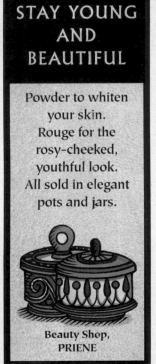

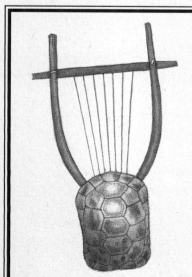
■ **1500–about 1150 B.C.**
Greece is divided into separate kingdoms, such as Mycenae. By about 1150 B.C., all of these kingdoms have collapsed.

■ **about 1100 B.C.**
Greek people first use iron.

■ **about 800 B.C.**
The Greek alphabet is first used by writers.

■ **about 800–700 B.C.**
City-states spring up all over Greece — small separate governments based on a single city or island.

■ **776 B.C.**
Earliest recorded date of the Olympic Games.

■ **700s–500s B.C.**
Greek city-states set up colonies around the Mediterranean and Black Sea coasts.

■ **about 600 B.C.**
First Greek coins made.

■ **560 B.C.**
Pisistratus becomes the first tyrant of Athens. His son Hippias is thrown out in 510 B.C.

■ **508 B.C.**
The start of democracy in Athens.

■ **499–490 B.C.**
The Persians invade Greece. In 490 B.C., they are beaten at the Battle of Marathon.

■ **480–479 B.C.**
The Persians invade Greece again. They are defeated at the battles of Salamis and Plataea.

■ **477–430s B.C.**
Led by Athens, many city-states unite to defend Greece from Persia. This group of city-states becomes the Athenian Empire.

■ **440s B.C.**
Athens is at the height of its power, under the leadership of Pericles. He remains Athens's most important politician until his death in 429 B.C.

■ **431 B.C.**
Sparta attacks Athens and starts the series of battles known as the Peloponnesian War.

■ **404 B.C.**
Sparta defeats Athens and becomes the most powerful city-state in Greece.

■ **369 B.C.**
Most of Sparta's land is conquered by the city-state of Thebes. Thebes remains the most powerful city-state until 362 B.C.

■ **338 B.C.**
The state of Macedonia comes to power when its king, Philip II, defeats the other Greek city-states.

■ **336 B.C.**
Philip II is murdered. His son Alexander the Great becomes ruler of Greece.

■ **334–326 B.C.**
Alexander invades Asia and conquers the vast Persian Empire.

■ **323 B.C.**
Alexander dies of a fever at Babylon. He has conquered Asia Minor, Egypt, Persia, and part of India. His empire is divided between his generals, and falls apart.

■ **170 B.C.**
A new power is growing to the west of Greece — the Roman Empire. By about 170 B.C., it controls all of Italy.

■ **146 B.C.**
All of the Greek city-states become part of the Roman Empire.

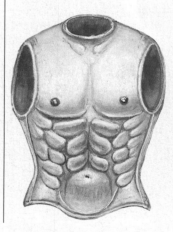

All of the dates in this book have the letters B.C. after them. B.C. stands for Before Christ — so 250 B.C., for example, means 250 years before the birth of Christ. The ancient Greeks did not count time in this way.

In this book, many of the country names are the ones we use today, such as France or Syria. The ancient Greeks would have used different names.

Authors: Anton Powell
Philip Steele
Consultant: Anton Powell,
Institute of Classics,
University of Wales

Advertisement illustrations by:
Katherine Baxter: 23br, 25tl, 27
Richard Berridge: 29br
Nicky Cooney: 18
Sarah Fox-Davies: 31bl
Maxine Hamil: 19bl, 23bl, 25bl, 25bm, 26br, 28br, 29bl, 30
Robbie Polley: 25br
George Thompson: 19br, 22r

Decorative borders by:
Nicky Cooney: 10, 11
Maxine Hamil: 8, 18, 19, 22, 25, 28, 29
Sue Shields: 20, 21

With thanks to:
Artist Partners, John Martin and Artists Ltd., Linden Artists Ltd., Specs Art, Virgil Pomfret Agency.

ISBN 0-590-05660-3
Text copyright © 1996 by Anton Powell and Philip Steele.
Illustrations copyright © 1996 by Walker Books Ltd.
All rights reserved. Published by Scholastic Inc., 555 Broadway, New York, NY 10012, by arrangement with Candlewick Press.

12 11 10 9 8 7 6 5 4 3 2 1
7 8 9/9 0 1 2/0

Printed in the U.S.A. 08
First Scholastic printing, January 1997

This book was typeset in Tiepolo.

First published by Candlewick Press

CANDLEWICK PRESS
2067 MASSACHUSETTS AVENUE
CAMBRIDGE MA 02140

In this book we have used the Roman spellings for names of places and people. In some books you will see the same names with Greek spellings, like the examples shown below.

Roman spellings	Greek spellings
Acropolis	Akropolis
Asclepius	Asklepios
Bucephalus	Boukephalos
Clisthenes	Kleisthenes
Croesus	Kroisos
Cyrene	Kyrene
Dionysus	Dionysos
Epidaurus	Epidauros
Hippocrates	Hippokrates
Miletus	Miletos
Mount Olympus	Mount Olympos
Pericles	Perikles
Pisistratus	Peisistratos
Socrates	Sokrates
Themistocles	Themistokles